This book belongs to:

Copyright © 2018 by Christian Art Kids,
an imprint of Christian Art Publishers,
PO Box 1599, Vereeniging, 1930, RSA

359 Longview Drive, Bloomingdale, IL 60108, USA

First edition 2018

Cover designed by Christian Art Kids

Images used under license from Shutterstock.com

Scripture quotations are taken from the *Holy Bible*, English Standard Version.
Copyright © 2001 by Crossway Bibles, a division of Good News Publishers.
Used by permission. All rights reserved.

Scripture quotations are taken from the *Holy Bible*,
New Living Translation®, first edition.
Copyright © 1996 by Tyndale House Publishers, Inc., Carol Stream,
Illinois 60188.

Scripture quotations are taken from the Contemporary English Version®.
Copyright © 1995 by American Bible Society.
All rights reserved.

Printed in China

ISBN 978-1-4321-2488-5

18 19 20 21 22 23 24 25 26 27 – 10 9 8 7 6 5 4 3 2 1

FAITH ABCs

CAROLYN LARSEN

christian
art kids

CONTENTS

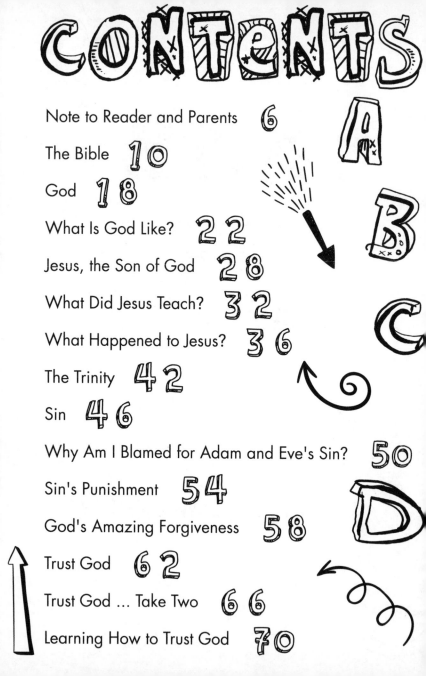

Note to Reader and Parents

Dear Reader

There are some words and phrases you may never hear except in relation to the Bible or the Christian life since they aren't used about many other things. This book is to help you understand some basic concepts of your Christian faith that are represented by those words. It explains terms that you may often hear or read about but do not fully understand.

You will likely have more questions after you read these explanations so talk with your parents or another trusted adult for help understanding. My prayer is that this book will help you grow closer to God and deeper in your faith in Him.

Blessings,

Carolyn Larsen

Dear Parents

This book is intended to be a first or second step in your child's understanding of the basics of Christian faith. It explains some of the basic terms that are a part of our faith vocabulary. It will hopefully open doors for further discussion with your child. The biblical story examples show how these concepts have been a part of living with God since the beginning.

Please understand that this book is not intended to be an "end all" on these topics. It should be a conversation starter for you and your child and an opportunity for further explanation from the perspective of your particular beliefs.

My prayer is for good conversation and deeper understanding for your precious children.

Blessings,

Carolyn Larsen

ABCs OF
BEING A CHRISTIAN

Be salt and light
Matthew 5:13-16

Always give thanks
1 Thessalonians 5:16-19

Count your blessings
Psalm 103:1-5

Do your best
Colossians 3:23

Encourage others
1 Thessalonians 5:11

Forgive others
Colossians 3:12-14

Give cheerfully
2 Corinthians 9:6-12

Honor your parents
Ephesians 6:2

Increase your faith
2 Peter 1:5-10

Jump for joy
Psalm 100:2

Kbe kind and caring
Ephesians 4:32

Love others
1 Corinthians 13:4-8

Make peace
Colossians 3:15

Never give up
Galatians 6:9

 Obey God
John 14:21

 Pray about everything
Philippians 4:6-7

 Quit complaining
Philippians 2:14-15

 Respect others
1 Peter 2:17

 Speak kindly
Proverbs 16:24

 Tell the truth
Ephesians 4:15-16

 Use your talents
1 Peter 4:10-11

 **V**ictorious in God
Psalm 18:29

 Wait on God
Psalm 27:14

e **X**alt God
Psalm 34:3

 Yield to Others
Philippians 2:3-4

 **Z**ealously share the Good News
Mark 16:15

THE BIBLE

YOUR WORD IS A LAMP TO GUIDE MY FEET AND A LIGHT FOR MY PATH.

PSALM 119:105

The Bible is the Word of God, written by men but inspired by God. That means He told men what to write. Why is that important? Because God's Word is His communication with His people. He wrote the Bible so that we can know how to live for Him; how to obey Him; how to treat other people and how to show God's love to others.

What do we learn from reading the Bible? We see how God shows love to His people. We see how He answers prayers. We learn that God is serious about being the only God in people's lives. He wants our full attention and obedience. He wants our love ... because He loves us.

The Bible is divided into sections. The 39 books of the Old Testament include books on law (Genesis through Deuteronomy); history books (Joshua through Esther); books of poetry (Job through Song of Solomon); major prophets (Isaiah through Daniel) and minor prophets (Hosea through Malachi).

The 27 books of the New Testament include the four gospels (Matthew through John); a book on the history of the church (Acts); letters of Paul (Romans through Philemon); general epistles (Hebrews through Jude) and prophecy (Revelation).

Look at the bookshelf on the next page to see how the Bible books are divided up.

Old Testament Books

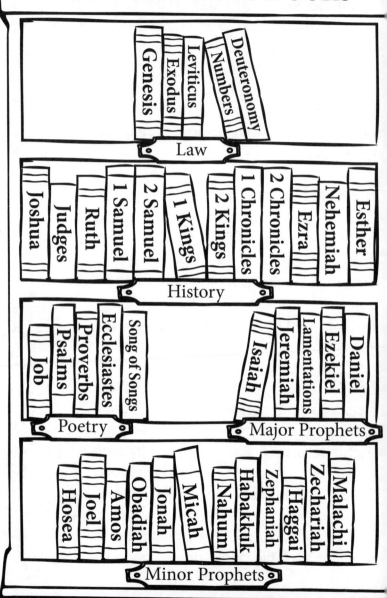

New Testament Books

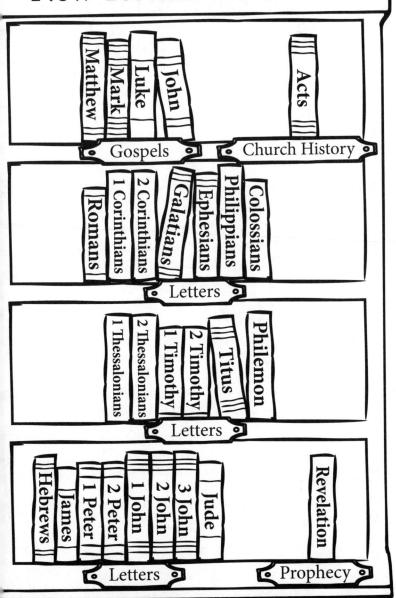

What does the Bible say?

Psalm 119:11

I have hidden Your word in my heart, that I might not sin against You.

Hebrews 4:12

For the word of God is alive and powerful. It is sharper than the sharpest two-edged sword, cutting between soul and spirit, between joint and marrow. It exposes our innermost thoughts and desires.

2 Timothy 3:16-17

All Scripture is inspired by God and is useful to teach us what is true and to make us realize what is wrong in our lives. It corrects us when we are wrong and teaches us to do what is right. God uses it to prepare and equip His people to do every good work.

Romans 15:4

The Scriptures were written to teach and encourage us by giving us hope.

Jesus quotes the Bible

Jesus went to the wilderness all by Himself. He didn't eat anything for 40 days and 40 nights and He became very hungry. Then the devil showed up. He said, "If You are really the Son of God, turn these stones into bread."

But Jesus answered, "People do not live by bread alone, but by every word that comes from the mouth of God."

Next the devil took Jesus to the highest spot of the temple in Jerusalem. He said, "If You are the Son of God, jump from here. The Scriptures say He will order His angels to protect You. And they will hold You up with their hands so You won't even hurt Your foot on a stone."

But Jesus said, "The Scriptures also say, 'You must not test the Lord your God.'"

Read the whole story in Matthew 4:1-11

Then the devil took Jesus to a high mountain and showed Him all the kingdoms of the world. "I'll give these all to You if You bow down and worship me," the devil said.

Jesus answered, "The Scriptures say, 'You must worship the Lord your God and serve only Him.'"

THE BIBLE IS:

Alive and Active
Hebrews 4:12

Sword

God-breathed
2 Timothy 3:16-17

Compass

Mirror

Lamp for my feet
Psalm 119:105

Map

Light on my path
Psalm 119:105

Daily bread
Matthew 4:4

I AM THE FIRST AND THE LAST; THERE IS NO OTHER GOD.

ISAIAH 44:6

The Christian faith begins with God. So, who is God? He is the Creator of everything there is. He is a Spirit. He is pure and holy. He is all powerful; nothing is stronger or more powerful than He is. He is complete in three persons: the Father, the Son (Jesus) and the Holy Spirit. He is present everywhere at the same time. He knows everything that happens. He will not share worship with any other being or idol. He is righteous and just and demands obedience but He loves all people and offers grace so that we get many, many chances to serve and obey Him. He is eternal – He has no beginning and no end.

God loves people and He wants people to know Him and accept His gifts of love and grace. He is always the same. He doesn't say one thing today and then changes His mind tomorrow. He can be trusted to guide you and you can always be sure of His love.

Is it easy to understand God? No. He is bigger and more powerful than our minds can understand. Accept His love, serve and obey Him. Read His Word and you will learn more and more about Him.

God is more powerful than our minds can understand!

What does the Bible say?

Genesis 1:1

In the beginning God created the heavens and the earth.

Exodus 20:5

"I, the LORD your God, am a jealous God who will not tolerate your affection for any other gods."

Malachi 3:6

"I am the LORD, and I do not change."

Psalm 147:5

How great is our Lord! His power is absolute! His understanding is beyond comprehension!

Matthew 19:26

Jesus looked at them intently and said, "Humanly speaking, it is impossible. But with God everything is possible."

Moses meets God
on Mt. Sinai

Moses went up on Mt. Sinai to have a private meeting with God. It was an amazing privilege for Moses, as the leader of the Israelite people. God gave very clear instructions about how to prepare the people for His presence to come near them. His specific instructions were evidence of His power and holiness.

Moses was to purify the people which means to make sure they confessed their sin. They were even instructed to wash their clothes. God said Moses should mark off a boundary around the bottom of the mountain and tell the people not to pass the boundary. They couldn't even touch the mountain or they would die!

On the day God came, thunder boomed and lightning flashed and a thick cloud covered the mountain. Moses led the people into God's presence; smoke covered everything and the people shook in fear. They recognized God's power and knew that He must be obeyed and worshiped.

Read more about it in Exodus 19

WHAT IS GOD LIKE?

"GOD IS SPIRIT,
SO THOSE WHO WORSHIP
HIM MUST WORSHIP IN
SPIRIT AND IN TRUTH."

JOHN 4:24

There are no photos of God or Jesus. We just have artists' impressions of Jesus – and they don't begin to show what He really looked like. So what do we actually know about God? How do we know what He is like?

Scripture tells us that God is a Spirit. He doesn't have flesh and blood like a person does. We also know that He has great wisdom, in fact, He knows everything. This is called omniscience. He is present everywhere at once. This is called omnipresence. He is awesome and worthy of worship. God is to be obeyed and worshiped and He responds to those who love, obey and worship Him with pure, unconditional love.

Another thing we know about God is that there are three persons to His presence. God the Father, God the Son (Jesus) and God the Holy Spirit. This is called the Trinity. They are all equal. They are all one.

If you think that this is not easy to understand, you are probably right. So, just be thankful for your God who loves you, knows everything about you, lives in your heart and will guide you, help you and protect you.

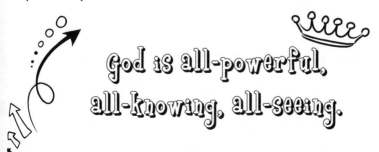

God is all-powerful, all-knowing, all-seeing.

What does the Bible say?

Psalm 86:5

O Lord, You are so good, so ready to forgive, so full of unfailing love for all who ask for Your help.

Psalm 139:7

I can never escape from Your Spirit! I can never get away from Your presence!

1 John 1:5

This is the message we heard from Jesus and now declare to you: God is light, and there is no darkness in Him at all.

Numbers 23:19

God is not a man, so He does not lie. He is not human, so He does not change His mind.

Lamentations 3:22-23

The faithful love of the LORD never ends! His mercies never cease. Great is His faithfulness; His mercies begin afresh each morning.

Our Gentle, Awesome God!

King Ahab and Queen Jezebel were very angry with Elijah. They thought it was his fault that no rain had fallen on their land in a long time. Elijah had to get away so he ran to Mt. Horeb to hide from them. God came to Elijah and asked him, "What are you doing here?"

Elijah said, "God, I've tried to serve You and teach the people about You. But they have torn down Your altars and killed all the other prophets. I'm the only one left and they are trying to kill me."

God said, "Go out of this cave and stand on the mountain and I will pass by you." Elijah went out of the cave and a wind blew that was so strong that rocks were torn out of the mountain. But God was not in the wind. Then there was a powerful earthquake but God was not in the earthquake either. Next was a blazing fire but God wasn't in the fire. Next was a gentle whisper. When Elijah heard the whisper, he knew that God was passing by. He covered his head with his coat and went to the door of the cave. God was in the whisper.

Read more about it in 1 Kings 19

YES!

Our God is an Awesome God!

JESUS, THE SON OF GOD

"THIS IS HOW GOD LOVED THE WORLD: HE GAVE HIS ONE AND ONLY SON, SO THAT EVERYONE WHO BELIEVES IN HIM WILL NOT PERISH BUT HAVE ETERNAL LIFE."

JOHN 3:16

Who is Jesus? He is God's only Son. Just like God the Father, He has always been, He has no beginning and no end. He had a part in the creation of the world. He was a willing part of God's answer to mankind's sin.

Jesus is God and is one Person of the Trinity. He has wisdom, power, and holiness just as His Father, God. He also has the same love for all people. So, Jesus left the glory of heaven and came to earth as a human baby. When He grew up He taught people about God. He lived the example of how to live for God and love Him. He did miracles that showed His godly power and His love for people when He healed their illnesses, brought loved ones back to life and forgave sins. That was all amazing, but the most amazing thing Jesus did was ... die.

Even though He had never sinned – never done anything wrong – He was arrested and murdered by His enemies and this was all part of God's plan. When Jesus died, He paid the price for all peoples' sins. His sacrifice of death became the bridge that makes a personal relationship with God possible for all of us.

What does the Bible say?

Matthew 3:17

A voice from heaven said, "This is My dearly loved Son, who brings Me great joy."

Isaiah 7:14

The Lord Himself will give you the sign. Look! The virgin will conceive a child! She will give birth to a son and will call Him Immanuel (which means 'God is with us').

Matthew 1:21

She will have a Son, and you are to name Him Jesus, for He will save His people from their sins.

John 14:6

Jesus told him, "I am the way, the truth, and the life. No one can come to the Father except through Me."

Romans 5:8

God showed His great love for us by sending Christ to die for us while we were still sinners.

The Birth of Jesus

Mary was just an average teenage girl when God's angel came to give her a special message. The angel said, "Mary, God is really happy with you. He has a special job He would like you to do. He says that you are going to have a baby boy. He will be a special baby because He is God's own Son."

Mary was confused because she wasn't even married. She was engaged to Joseph. But she loved God very much and she tried to serve and obey Him. So, she listened to the angel's message and then said, "I will do whatever God wants."

A few months later Joseph and Mary were in Bethlehem because the ruler wanted a count of all the people who lived in his country. The town was crowded so the only place Joseph could find for them to stay was in a stable with the animals. While they were there, Mary's special baby was born. God's angel appeared to shepherds in a field outside of town and said, "Today your Savior has been born!" The shepherds hurried into town to find the special baby and worship Him.

Read more about this in **Luke 2**

WHAT DID JESUS TEACH?

ONE DAY AS HE SAW THE CROWDS GATHERING, JESUS WENT UP ON THE MOUNTAINSIDE AND SAT DOWN. HIS DISCIPLES GATHERED AROUND HIM, AND HE BEGAN TO TEACH THEM.

MATTHEW 5:1-2

Jesus is God's Son. When He came to earth it was because of God's plan to make a way for people to know Him and have a personal friendship with Him. When Jesus died He paid for the sins of all people, even though He had never sinned at all. That made it possible for us all to know God personally. God raised Jesus back to life and that miracle was evidence of the promise that all who accept Jesus as Savior will live with Him forever in heaven.

But Jesus did not come to earth just to die for our sins. He also came to teach people how to live together in peace and love and how to know God better. He taught about living for God in ways that the people had never heard before. What He taught showed people how much God loved them.

One of Jesus' best-known sermons is found in the Sermon on the Mount in Matthew 5. It's called that because He and His followers were sitting together on a mountain when Jesus taught them how people should treat one another and how they should love God with all their hearts.

SALT & LIGHT
MATTHEW 5:13-16

What does the Bible say?

Matthew 5:9

"God blesses those who work for peace, for they will be called the children of God."

Matthew 5:14

"You are the light of the world – like a city on a hilltop that cannot be hidden."

Matthew 5:22

"If you are even angry with someone, you are subject to judgment! If you call someone an idiot, you are in danger of being brought before the court. And if you curse someone, you are in danger of the fires of hell."

Matthew 5:39

"If someone slaps you on the right cheek, offer the other cheek also."

Matthew 5:44

"I say, love your enemies! Pray for those who persecute you!"

The Sermon
on the Mount

A crowd of people followed Jesus everywhere He went. One day the large crowd around Him sat down on the side of a mountain to hear Jesus teach. The lessons Jesus taught that day are recorded in Matthew 5 through chapter 7 and are called The Sermon on the Mount. The main theme of this sermon is the call to righteousness, which means obeying God and doing His will. Jesus teaches how to do that in this sermon.

A main part of the Sermon on the Mount is the blessings that Jesus outlines. These are called the Beatitudes and are found in verses 3-12 of Matthew chapter 5. Jesus describes God's blessings to His people and encourages those who are suffering to remember that God knows and cares about them.

Jesus also taught about handling your anger or wanting to get revenge on those who hurt you. He taught about loving your enemies and helping people who need things. The Sermon covers teaching about prayer, worry and judging others.

You can learn a lot about obeying God by reading the Sermon on the Mount.

You can read all about it in Matthew 5-7

WHAT HAPPENED TO JESUS?

TWO OTHERS, BOTH CRIMINALS, WERE LED OUT TO BE EXECUTED WITH HIM. WHEN THEY CAME TO A PLACE CALLED THE SKULL, THEY NAILED HIM TO THE CROSS. AND THE CRIMINALS WERE ALSO CRUCIFIED - ONE ON HIS RIGHT AND ONE ON HIS LEFT.

LUKE 23:32-33

Jesus taught people how to live for God and how to treat other people. He healed sick folks and even raised some dead people back to life. He did good things. He never did anything wrong ... not even once.

Jesus did His work on earth for about three-and-a-half years. That whole time He was traveling around teaching about God and healing sick people. He wanted to reach as many people as possible.

As Jesus' popularity grew, the religious leaders (called Pharisees) got more and more angry with Him. They knew He was becoming very popular with people because a crowd followed Him everywhere He went. He was teaching people to know God and worship God without following all the laws the Pharisees insisted they follow.

Finally the Pharisees had enough. They came up with a plan to get rid of Jesus. They made false accusations against Him and even got people to agree with them. Finally Jesus was arrested, a quick middle of the night trial was held and He was sentenced to death. This all happened before the people even really knew what was going on. The Pharisees succeeded in killing an innocent Man, but things weren't over ... God wasn't finished!

What does the Bible say?

Luke 23:46

Jesus shouted, "Father, I entrust My spirit into Your hands!" And with those words He breathed His last.

John 3:16

"For this is how God loved the world: He gave His one and only Son, so that everyone who believes in Him will not perish but have eternal life."

Philippians 2:6-8

Though He was God, He did not think of equality with God as something to cling to. Instead, He gave up His divine privileges; He took the humble position of a slave and was born as a human being. When He appeared in human form, He humbled Himself in obedience to God and died a criminal's death on a cross.

Romans 5:8

God showed His great love for us by sending Christ to die for us while we were still sinners.

Jesus' Death and Resurrection

Late one night the Pharisees had Jesus arrested while He and His followers were in the Garden of Gethsemane. Jesus had warned His disciples that this was going to happen. A quick trial was held in the middle of the night and Jesus was sentenced to death by crucifixion. He was nailed to a wooden cross and He hung there until He died. When Jesus died, He paid the penalty for the sins of all mankind. Any person who will accept Him as Savior will receive the gift of being saved from the punishment of sin.

The day Jesus died; His enemies thought they had won. Jesus was buried in a donated tomb and guards stood by to make sure no one stole His body so that it would look like God had raised Him back to life. This all happened on Friday.

Sunday morning some women went to the tomb to put special oils and perfumes on Jesus' body. But, when they got there they found that the tomb was empty. At first they thought His body had been stolen, but then they found out that God had raised Jesus back to life! God had won and showed His followers that the promise of eternal life was real!

Read more about it in **John 18:1-20**

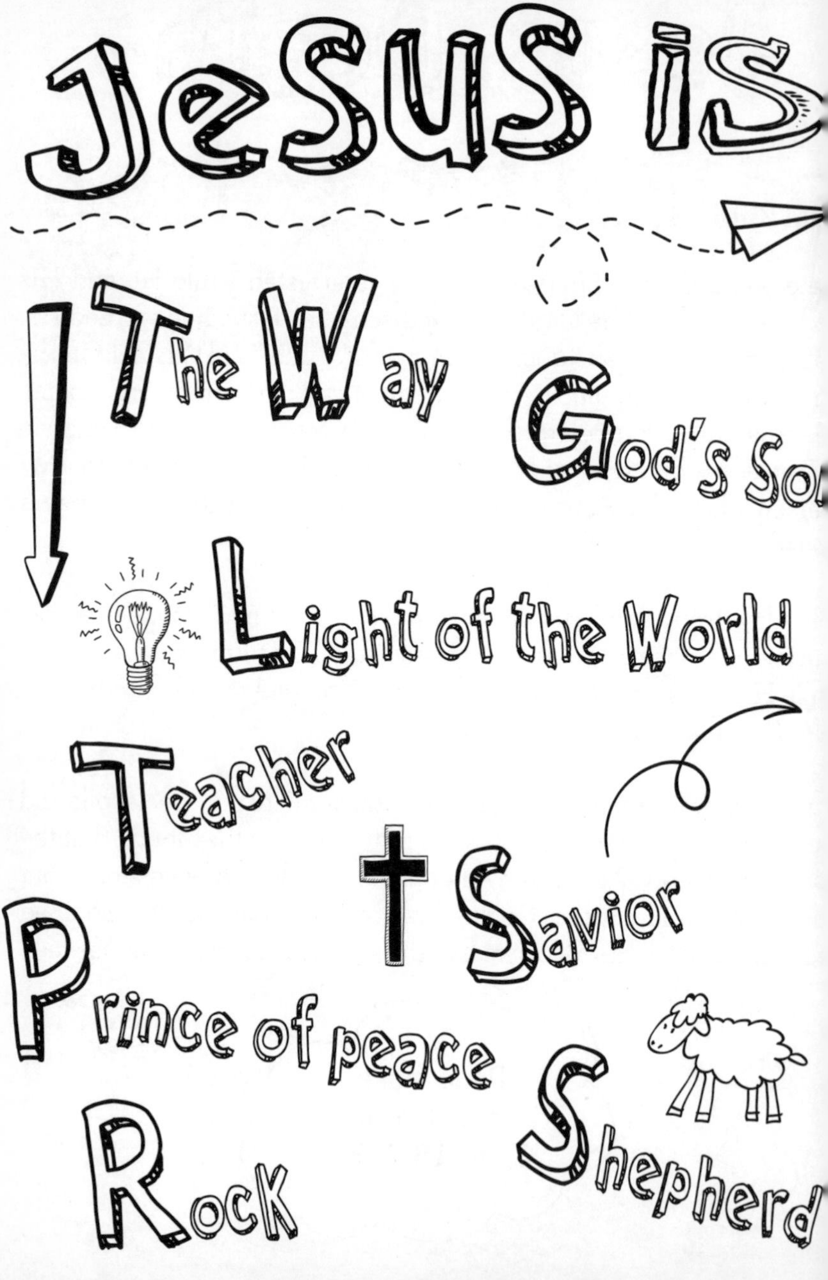

JeSUS iS

The Way

God's So[n]

Light of the World

Teacher

✝ Savior

Prince of peace

Rock

Shepherd

THE TRINITY

AFTER HIS BAPTISM, AS JESUS CAME UP OUT OF THE WATER, THE HEAVENS WERE OPENED AND HE SAW THE SPIRIT OF GOD DESCENDING LIKE A DOVE AND SETTLING ON HIM. AND A VOICE FROM HEAVEN SAID, "THIS IS MY DEARLY LOVED SON, WHO BRINGS ME GREAT JOY"

MATTHEW 3:16-17

The Trinity is not an easy topic to understand. The word *Trinity* is not found in the Bible but we use it to describe the three Persons of God who are described in the Bible – God the Father, God the Son (Jesus), and God the Holy Spirit. Understand that there is only ONE God, not three. He is described in the Bible using these three titles – God the Father, the Son and the Holy Spirit. So, Bible teachers came up with the word Trinity – three parts of the whole. Each of the three have certain tasks:

✝ The Father is the One who was in charge of creating everything. He is also the source of our salvation.

✝ God, the Son is the One who God the Father works through for creation and salvation.

✝ God the Holy Spirit is the power that God uses for creating the universe and keeping it going, for revelation or communication with mankind and Jesus' works.

Each member of the Trinity is God. They cannot be separated. While this is a hard thing to understand, there are verses in the Bible that describe each of these Persons.

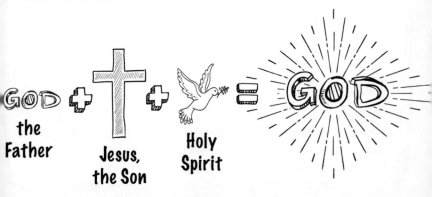

GOD
the Father

Jesus, the Son

Holy Spirit

= GOD

What does the Bible say?

Matthew 28:19

"Therefore, go and make disciples of all the nations, baptizing them in the name of the Father and the Son and the Holy Spirit."

Deuteronomy 6:4

Listen, O Israel! The Lord is our God, the Lord alone.

John 15:26

"I will send you the Advocate – the Spirit of truth. He will come to you from the Father and will testify all about Me."

2 Corinthians 13:14

May the grace of the Lord Jesus Christ, the love of God, and the fellowship of the Holy Spirit be with you all.

1 John 5:20

We know that the Son of God has come, and He has given us understanding so that we can know the true God. And now we live in fellowship with the true God because we live in fellowship with His Son, Jesus Christ. He is the only true God, and He is eternal life.

The Coming of the Holy Spirit

While Jesus was doing His work on earth, people depended on Him to teach them the right way to live for God. But when He knew that He was going to die, He promised to send His followers a Comforter – the Holy Spirit.

Jesus was crucified, buried and three days later He rose back to life. A few of His followers saw Him and talked with Him but then He went to heaven. That all happened and no Comforter had come.

One day Jesus' followers were together in a room. Suddenly a sound filled the room like a strong wind. Everyone saw something that looked like little flames of fire float through the air and hang in the air above each person's head. When that happened every person in the room was filled with the power of the Holy Spirit – the Comforter!

People came running to see what was going on and the men in the room were suddenly able to speak in languages other than their own. So, everyone who came could understand someone in the room!

No one understood what was happening so Peter stood up and began to explain. He told them that Jesus' promise had just been kept and the Holy Spirit of God, the Comforter, had come!

Read more about it in Acts 2

45

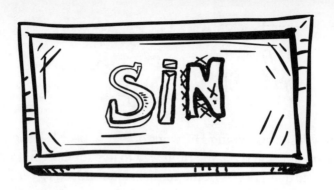

EVERYONE WHO SINS IS BREAKING GOD'S LAW, FOR ALL SIN IS CONTRARY TO THE LAW OF GOD.

1 JOHN 3:4

Sin – a little word that packs a big wallop. When sin became part of the world everything changed. The Bible says that every person who lives is a sinner ... except Jesus. Do you wonder what sin actually is?

The Bible says that sin is anything that breaks God's laws. God says, "Don't lie" so when you tell a lie – even a little one, that's sin. God says He should be most important in your life. God says, "Don't be jealous of others, don't be full of pride, don't cheat, be kind, be honest, love others." So, if you do the opposite of any of those things – that's sin.

Sin began with the first people, Adam and Eve. God made a beautiful place for them to live and He gave them one rule – don't eat the fruit of this one tree. The devil tempted Eve and she ate that fruit. Adam tasted it too. They disobeyed God. That was the beginning of sin. Sin breaks your relationship with God, but He had a plan for forgiveness. We'll talk about that soon.

What does the Bible say?

Romans 3:23

Everyone has sinned; we all fall short of God's glorious standard.

James 4:17

Remember, it is sin to know what you ought to do and then not do it.

Ecclesiastes 7:20

Not a single person on earth is always good and never sins.

Romans 8:8

Those who are still under the control of their sinful nature can never please God.

Isaiah 59:12

For our sins are piled up before God and testify against us. Yes, we know what sinners we are.

The First Sin

God made Adam, the first man. He used one of Adam's ribs to make Eve, the first woman. God put everything they needed to live in the Garden of Eden. He said they could eat any fruit in the garden – except the fruit of one tree ... the Tree of the Knowledge of Good and Evil. They were not to even touch that tree.

But one day a sneaky snake (which was actually the devil in disguise) slithered up to Eve and spoke, "Did God really say you can't eat that fruit?" he asked.

"Yes," Eve said, "God said that if we eat that fruit or even touch it, we will die."

"You won't really die," the snake said. He convinced Eve. She tasted the fruit and then gave some to Adam. He ate it, too. They disobeyed God. That was the first sin.

Read the whole story in **Genesis 3**

49

WHY AM I BLAMED FOR ADAM AND EVE'S SIN?

EVERYONE HAS SINNED; WE ALL FALL SHORT OF GOD'S GLORIOUS STANDARD.

ROMANS 3:23

Sin began when Adam and Eve disobeyed God. God gave people the freedom to make choices. People can choose to obey Him or not. Adam and Eve chose to disobey God. But why did that make all people for the rest of time sinners, too? Because God saw that the weaknesses and self-centeredness in Adam and Eve would be true of all humans forever. We would make choices that do not always honor Him. Sin became a part of human DNA after that first sin.

Even if you don't want to sin; even if you try not to, you will. You can't help it. That doesn't mean that God turns away from you. It doesn't mean He won't forgive you or that He doesn't love you. But sin breaks your relationship with God because He is completely sinless and pure. He can't have anything to do with sin.

Before the first sin even happened, God already had a plan to fix the broken relationship between sinful people and Himself. God sent His Son, Jesus, to pay the price for sin and to be the bridge that makes a relationship with God possible for any who accepts Jesus as their Savior.

Christ's Payment

Man's Problem: Sin

Eternal Life with God

Sin's Penalty: Death

Eternal Death

What does the Bible say?

James 4:4

Don't you realize that friendship with the world makes you an enemy of God? I say it again: If you want to be a friend of the world, you make yourself an enemy of God.

Luke 6:45

"A good person produces good things from the treasury of a good heart, and an evil person produces evil things from the treasury of an evil heart. What you say flows from what is in your heart."

1 John 1:6

We are lying if we say we have fellowship with God but go on living in spiritual darkness; we are not practicing the truth.

Romans 7:19-20

I want to do what is good, but I don't. I don't want to do what is wrong, but I do it anyway. But if I do what I don't want to do, I am not really the one doing wrong; it is sin living in me that does it.

Basics of Sin

The Israelites were God's people. He loved them and wanted them to learn how to obey Him. So, He called Moses to come up on Mt. Sinai and He gave him the Ten Commandments. They would help the people learn how to live for God and obey Him. The people needed the guidance of these commandments so they could really understand what they were doing wrong. Once they heard the commands, they saw the many ways they disobeyed by how they treated Him and other people.

The Ten Commandments helped the Israelites learn how to obey God:

Read the whole story in **Exodus 20**

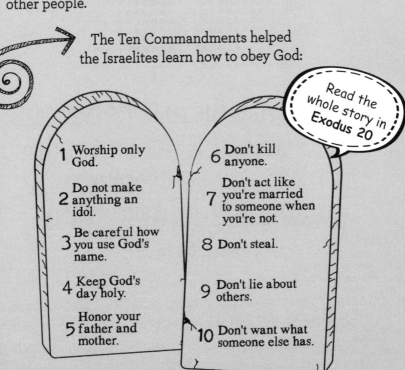

1 Worship only God.

2 Do not make anything an idol.

3 Be careful how you use God's name.

4 Keep God's day holy.

5 Honor your father and mother.

6 Don't kill anyone.

7 Don't act like you're married to someone when you're not.

8 Don't steal.

9 Don't lie about others.

10 Don't want what someone else has.

SIN'S PUNISHMENT

THE WAGES OF SIN IS DEATH, BUT THE FREE GIFT OF GOD IS ETERNAL LIFE THROUGH CHRIST JESUS OUR LORD.

ROMANS 6:23

Here's what we know – sin is bad but you can't help sinning, no matter how hard you try. Since sin is disobedience to God it breaks your relationship with Him. If you don't ask His forgiveness and His help to stop sinning, you will be punished. The punishment is serious.

Romans 6:23 says that the punishment for sin is death. Yikes, does that mean you will fall down dead because you sin – sin that you can't stop doing no matter how hard you try? No, the death that this verse talks about is not an immediate, physical death.

God made a way for the forgiveness of sin. His Son, Jesus, came to earth and died to pay the price for your sin. So, if you do not confess your sins to God and ask forgiveness; if you do not accept Jesus as your Savior who paid the price for your sin, then you will be separated from God forever. You will not be able to enter His heaven when you leave this earth. You will spend forever in hell, away from God. That's the punishment and that's true death.

Accept Jesus as your Savior

What does the Bible say?

James 1:15

These desires give birth to sinful actions. And when sin is allowed to grow, it gives birth to death.

Romans 5:12

When Adam sinned, sin entered the world. Adam's sin brought death, so death spread to everyone, for everyone sinned.

Acts 3:19

Repent of your sins and turn to God, so that your sins may be wiped away.

John 3:16

This is how God loved the world: He gave His one and only Son, so that everyone who believes in Him will not perish but have eternal life.

1 John 1:9

If we confess our sins to Him, He is faithful and just to forgive us our sins and to cleanse us from all wickedness.

Punishment

No one can say that he is not a sinner because God says everyone is. God also says that the punishment for sin is death, which means the sinner cannot come into God's heaven but when he dies he will spend forever in hell, far away from God.

The way God provided salvation from the punishment of sin is that He sent His Son, Jesus, to earth. Jesus was killed and He took the punishment for the sins of all people. To accept this salvation instead of punishment, you must confess that you are a sinner, ask God's forgiveness and accept Jesus as your Savior from sin. Then, your punishment is gone – Jesus took it.

When Jesus was crucified on a cross, there were two thieves who were crucified on crosses on either side of Him. Neither of them had admitted they were sinners. Neither believed Jesus was God's Son and their Savior. They heard the things Jesus said while He was dying. One thief made fun of Jesus by saying bad things about Him. The other one believed that Jesus was God's Son and asked His forgiveness. Jesus did forgive him and then when Jesus died, He took that man's punishment for sin.

Read the whole story in Luke 23:32-43

GOD'S AMAZING FORGIVENESS

WITHOUT THE SHEDDING OF BLOOD, THERE IS NO FORGIVENESS.

HEBREWS 9:22

God will happily forgive your sin ... but there is a requirement. There has always been a requirement – the shedding of blood. He requires a blood sacrifice from people who want to repent of their sin and be forgiven. Before Jesus came people would sacrifice animals to get the blood for the sacrifice. But then Jesus came and He was crucified – His blood was spilled to be the blood sacrifice for all people for all time.

God hates sin but He loves sinners ... people. Once you have accepted Jesus as your Savior, His blood pays for your sin ... you are forgiven forever.

When you sin again throughout life, confess it to God, tell Him you're truly sorry and He will forgive you. The goal, of course, is that as you learn to know God better and grow closer to Him, you will learn to be more like Him and sinless.

But, as that growth happens, know that your sin is always forgiven. Stay close to God, ask His forgiveness and remember to thank Him for the wonderful gift of Jesus.

What does the Bible say?

1 Peter 3:18

Christ suffered for our sins once for all time. He never sinned, but He died for sinners to bring you safely home to God. He suffered physical death, but He was raised to life in the Spirit.

Ephesians 1:7

He is so rich in kindness and grace that He purchased our freedom with the blood of His Son and forgave our sins.

Psalm 32:1-2

Oh, what joy for those whose disobedience is forgiven, whose sin is put out of sight! Yes, what joy for those whose record the LORD has cleared of guilt, whose lives are lived in complete honesty!

Psalm 103:12

He has removed our sins as far from us as the east is from the west.

An Example of
Forgiveness

Jesus told a story about God's forgiveness. He gave an example that people could understand:

A man had two sons. The older son was happy to work with his dad but the younger son was not happy. He dreamed of leaving home and living in the city on his own. So, he asked for his share of the money he would have coming to him when his father died so he could leave home.

His dad was sad to see his son leave but he gave him the money. The boy hurried to the city and wasted his money on parties and wild living. Pretty soon he was out of money. All the people he thought were friends disappeared and he had to get a job just to have food. The only job he could find was feeding pigs. He got so hungry he ate the pigs' food!

Pretty soon he remembered his father. He knew he had hurt his dad so he thought that he didn't deserve to be treated like a son but he hoped his dad would give him a job – he would be his father's servant.

He headed home, ready to beg his dad to let him be a servant, but when his father saw him coming, he ran to meet him. Before the boy could say anything his father welcomed him home with a big hug. All was forgiven.

Read the whole story in Luke 15:11-32

TRUST GOD

TRUST IN THE LORD WITH ALL YOUR HEART.

PROVERBS 3:5

What's the big deal about trusting God?

Trust is a big deal because it's impossible to have a relationship with God if you don't trust Him. Is it possible to believe He loves you and will take care of you if you don't trust Him?

It's easy to say you trust God. Like, "Yeah, I know God loves me and will take care of me blah, blah, blah." But, what's hard is to honestly trust Him – to believe He loves you, is looking out for you, could stop bad things from happening, knows what's going on and has a plan for your life. Really, honestly believe all that. How do you do it?

Trusting God means you believe He's good and He wants good things for you. It means believing He's dependable so you can trust what the Bible says. It means you believe He's looking out for you even when things get tough. So, even when you don't understand why hard things are happening, even when you're confused about stuff … you trust Him.

What does the Bible say?

Luke 12:22-23, 30-31

Jesus said, "That is why I tell you not to worry about everyday life – whether you have enough food to eat or enough clothes to wear. For life is more than food, and your body more than clothing. Your Father already knows your needs. Seek the kingdom of God above all else, and He will give you everything you need."

Psalm 9:10

Those who know Your name trust in You, for You, O LORD, do not abandon those who search for You.

Psalm 28:7

The LORD is my strength and shield. I trust Him with all my heart. He helps me, and my heart is filled with joy. I burst out in songs of thanksgiving.

Proverbs 3:5-6

Trust in the LORD with all your heart; do not depend on your own understanding. Seek His will in all you do, and He will show you which path to take.

Gideon Trusts God

The Midianites were enemies of the Israelites so they captured them and made them slaves! But God knew what was happening. He chose Gideon to lead the Israelite army and fight the Midianites to free God's people from slavery.

The Midianite army had 135,000 soldiers. Gideon only had 32,000 soldiers. So he was surprised when God said, "You have too many soldiers. Let anyone who is afraid go home." Gideon was left with just 10,000 soldiers. But God wasn't finished. He sent the 10,000 soldiers to a river to get a drink. Only the men who scooped up water in their hands and lapped it up like a dog were allowed to stay. After that, Gideon only had 300 soldiers left!

Would Gideon trust God's plan?

Yes! Gideon trusted God and his 300 men defeated 135,000 men without even one battle!

Read the whole story in Judges 7

"I KNOW THE PLANS I HAVE FOR YOU," SAYS THE LORD. "THEY ARE PLANS FOR GOOD AND NOT FOR DISASTER, TO GIVE YOU A FUTURE AND A HOPE."

JEREMIAH 29:11

Maybe you get that you need to trust God ... great! But, umm, what about when a bully picks on you or you ask God to help you win a soccer game, but you lose the game. What if someone you love gets sick or what about if your parents split up? Where's God when all these things happen? How are you supposed to trust God when He lets bad things happen?

News flash ... trusting God does NOT mean bad things will never happen. That would be nice, but it's not what the Christian life is all about. OK, so then what's the point of trusting Him?

The fact is that God does not promise to make your life easier. Sometimes stuff is hard. But what matters to God is that you learn to become more like Jesus. That means that even when you go through hard things you trust God to help you be brave, patient, kind and peaceful ... like Jesus. That's His plan for your life. That's why you should trust Him.

NEWS FLASH!
GOD HAS A PLAN FOR YOUR LIFE!

What does the Bible say?

Psalm 56:3

When I am afraid, I will put my trust in You.

Isaiah 12:2

God has come to save me. I will trust in Him and not be afraid. The LORD God is my strength and my song; He has given me victory.

Isaiah 43:1

But now, O Jacob, listen to the LORD who created you. O Israel, the one who formed you says, "Do not be afraid, for I have ransomed you. I have called you by name; you are Mine."

John 14:1

"Don't let your hearts be troubled. Trust in God, and trust also in Me."

Joseph Trusts God

Jacob had twelve sons but Joseph was his favorite. Joseph's brothers were jealous of Joseph and the gifts Jacob gave him. One day they decided to get rid of their brother. They sold him to slave traders on their way to Egypt and told their father that a wild animal killed his favorite son.

Joseph trusted God and that didn't change when he became a slave. He trusted God's plan for him. Soon he was put in charge of all the slaves in the house. His trust in God had another test when someone lied about him and he was thrown in jail! Soon Joseph was put in charge of all the prisoners. He kept trusting God and one day he was taken out of jail and made second in command of the whole country – all because he trusted God through hard times!

Read the whole story in **Genesis 37-50**

LEARNING HOW TO TRUST GOD

EVERY WORD OF GOD PROVES TRUE. HE IS A SHIELD TO ALL WHO COME TO HIM FOR PROTECTION.

PROVERBS 30:5

TRUST GOD. Does it frustrate you to hear that because you know it isn't easy to do? Are you afraid to admit your frustration because you don't know how God would feel about it? OK, that makes sense. Trusting God is obviously important, so the question is ... how do you learn to do it?

One simple way of learning to trust God is by reading the Bible. Why is that helpful? Think about it – the better you know another person, the easier it is to trust him.

Reading the Bible helps you get to know God because you read how He takes care of His people and how much He loves you.

The stories in the Bible teach you to obey Him and then trust Him to do what He says He will do … love, guide, protect and yes, even punish. His Word is true. He doesn't lie.

He wants to be involved in your life because He loves you – enough to sacrifice His only Son for your life. You have to trust someone who loves you so much!

What does the Bible say?

Psalm 33:4

For the word of the LORD holds true, and we can trust everything He does.

Isaiah 41:10

"Don't be afraid, for I am with you. Don't be discouraged, for I am your God. I will strengthen you and help you. I will hold you up with My victorious right hand."

Psalm 119:165

Those who love Your instructions have great peace and do not stumble.

Isaiah 40:31

Those who trust in the LORD will find new strength. They will soar high on wings like eagles. They will run and not grow weary. They will walk and not faint.

Jesus Read the Bible

Jesus didn't have the New Testament when He lived on earth. But He had the part we call the Old Testament. Jesus knew the Scriptures. He read it and quoted from it often. When the devil was tempting Him, He said, "The Scriptures say, 'People do not live by bread alone, but by every word that comes from the mouth of God.'" He was saying that knowing God's Word is important in order to know Him and live for Him.

One of Jesus' most famous teachings is the Sermon on the Mount. He quoted from the Old Testament many times in it. For example, "You have heard the law that says, 'Love your neighbor' and hate your enemy. But I say, love your enemies! Pray for those who persecute you!"

If reading the Bible was important enough for Jesus to do, then it surely must still be important for us!

Read more in **Matthew 4 and 5**

THIS IS HOW GOD LOVED THE WORLD: HE GAVE HIS ONE AND ONLY SON, SO THAT EVERYONE WHO BELIEVES IN HIM WILL NOT PERISH BUT HAVE ETERNAL LIFE.

JOHN 3:16

What does *Salvation* mean? The punishment for sin is eternal death, which means being separated from God's presence forever. Since every person is a sinner does that mean no one can have a relationship with God or be His friend? Never fear – God had a plan! He loves people and He wants everyone to know His love and be saved from punishment. So, He sent His Son, Jesus to earth. Jesus taught people how to know God. He helped people. He did good things and never sinned. NOT ONCE. Still, He was arrested and murdered. That was God's plan because when Jesus died, He took on Himself the punishment for all sins – for all time!

When you believe that Jesus did that and accept His gift of salvation He becomes your Savior – He saved you from the punishment of sin. Accepting Jesus as Savior means He is invited to live in your heart – to become your guide and conscience and ... well ... your helper day in and day out. He took your punishment because He loves you. He wants you to know Him, which is why He saved you.

What does the Bible say?

Romans 10:9-10

If you openly declare that Jesus is Lord and believe in your heart that God raised Him from the dead, you will be saved. For it is by believing in your heart that you are made right with God, and it is by openly declaring your faith that you are saved.

Acts 2:21

Everyone who calls on the name of the LORD will be saved.

Ephesians 2:8

God saved you by His grace when you believed. And you can't take credit for this; it is a gift from God.

Romans 5:8-9

But God showed His great love for us by sending Christ to die for us while we were still sinners. And since we have been made right in God's sight by the blood of Christ, He will certainly save us from God's condemnation.

The Woman
at the Well

Jesus and His friends were on the way to Galilee when they went into town to get food and He stopped by a well for a drink. There was a woman at the well, too, and Jesus asked her for a drink. She was from Samaria and Samaritans and Jews did not like each other so her response to His request was not very nice. But Jesus didn't get upset with her; He just told her that if she knew who she was talking to, she would be asking Him for the living water He could give her.

The woman was interested in the idea of living water because then she would never get thirsty again. But Jesus explained that this water was different from the water she could get from the well, it was water that would let her live forever. He told her that He was the Messiah whom people had been waiting for!

Right then and there the woman believed that Jesus was God's Son and she was saved.

Read the whole story in **John 4:5-42**

THE GIFT OF SALVATION

HE HAS REMOVED OUR SINS AS FAR FROM US AS THE EAST IS FROM THE WEST.

PSALM 103:12

Sometimes when you get into an argument with someone they might bring up some situation that happened a while ago – something you thought was completely settled and forgiven a long time ago. But when it comes up again, you know it wasn't settled and you weren't forgiven. It wasn't really gone. You don't have to worry about that with God. He forgives your sin and then He forgets it. He moves your sin far away from you so it isn't even a part of you anymore. The blessing of salvation is that

God focuses on today, not yesterday. He doesn't keep a list of your past sins that have already been confessed and forgiven. He won't throw them in your face again. Those sins are ancient history. They are gone. Thank God for His forgiveness that comes with your salvation. Thank Him that when you confess your sins, He forgives them and they are GONE!

LORD, THANK YOU FOR FORGIVING MY SIN AND FORGETTING ABOUT IT!

ABCs OF SALVATION

A dmit that you are a sinner

For everyone has sinned; we all fall short of God's glorious standard.

Romans 3:23

Believe that Jesus paid for your sin at the cross

or the wages of sin is death, but the free gift of od is eternal life through Christ Jesus our Lord.

Romans 6:23

But God showed His great love for us by sending Christ to die for us while we were still sinners.

Romans 5:8

Confess that Jesus is the Son of God and commit your life to Him.

If you declare with your mouth, "Jesus is Lord," and believe in your heart that God raised Him from the dead, you will be saved.

Romans 10:9

What does the Bible say?

Matthew 11:28

Jesus said, "Come to Me, all of you who are weary and carry heavy burdens, and I will give you rest."

Psalm 55:22

Give your burdens to the LORD, and He will take care of you. He will not permit the godly to slip and fall.

Isaiah 1:18

"Come now, let's settle this," says the LORD. "Though your sins are like scarlet, I will make them as white as snow. Though they are red like crimson, I will make them as white as wool."

Colossians 1:13-14

He has rescued us from the kingdom of darkness and transferred us into the Kingdom of His dear Son, who purchased our freedom and forgave our sins.

Story of Zacchaeus

No one liked Zacchaeus. He was a tax collector who had a habit of charging people more than they actually owed. He kept the extra money for himself. He stole from people and he didn't even care. Then Zacchaeus heard that Jesus was coming to his town and he wanted to see Him. The road was lined with crowds of people who also wanted to see Jesus. Zacchaeus was so short that he couldn't see over the crowd. So, how could he see Jesus? He had a brilliant idea! Zacchaeus climbed up a tree and he could see Jesus walking down the street below him.

Zacchaeus was very surprised when Jesus stopped right below the tree he was sitting in. "Zacchaeus," Jesus said, "come down. I want to come to your house today." Zacchaeus hurried down the tree and took Jesus to his house.

The people were amazed that Jesus would visit with such an awful sinner as Zacchaeus. What they didn't know is that after talking to Jesus, Zacchaeus said he was sorry for stealing from people and he promised to pay back four times what he had stolen. Jesus said, "Salvation has come to this house today."

Read the whole story in Luke 19:1-10

THE SACRIFICE OF LOVE

"THERE IS NO GREATER LOVE THAN TO LAY DOWN ONE'S LIFE FOR ONE'S FRIENDS."

JOHN 15:13

In Old Testament times the people had to offer animal sacrifices at the temple when they came to ask God's forgiveness for their sins and to worship Him. That means that an animal had to be killed. God required the shedding of blood. Anyone who came to ask forgiveness and worship God had to make an animal sacrifice.

Then Jesus, God's own Son, came to earth. He

taught people how to live for God and obey Him. He did miracles of healing sick people and even raising dead people back to life.

Then Jesus was arrested and condemned to die even though He had never done anything wrong. Jesus was nailed to a cross and hung there until He died. His own blood that flowed as He died became the sacrifice for all people's sins from that moment on. This was God's plan all along. He made a way for people to have a friendship with Him. That's how much God loves people.

We no longer have to sacrifice an animal as we ask forgiveness for our sins. Jesus died for our sins and that was a sacrifice of love.

What does the Bible say?

Romans 5:8

God showed His great love for us by sending Christ to die for us while we were still sinners.

1 John 2:2

He Himself is the sacrifice that atones for our sins – and not only our sins but the sins of all the world.

Ephesians 5:2

Live a life filled with love, following the example of Christ. He loved us and offered Himself as a sacrifice for us, a pleasing aroma to God.

Leviticus 17:11

The life of the body is in its blood. I have given you the blood on the altar to purify you, making you right with the LORD. It is the blood, given in exchange for a life, that makes purification possible.

Hebrews 9:12

With His own blood – not the blood of goats and calves – He entered the Most Holy Place once for all time and secured our redemption forever.

Love's Sacrifice

God has one Son ... only one – Jesus. God and Jesus together came up with the plan for the sacrifice of love that makes salvation possible. The plan was in place a long time before it happened. You will know that by reading verses in the Old Testament that were written a long time before Jesus was even born. These verses are called "prophecy." Prophecy tells us what will happen in the future.

Isaiah chapter 53 in the Old Testament reveals that Jesus, who grew up in God's presence would come to earth and be rejected by the very people He came to help. He would suffer, be arrested, tried and killed like a common criminal. These verses in Isaiah say that this Man's life would be given as a ransom for many. That means Jesus' life was sacrificed so that all people's sins could be forgiven. God and Jesus came up with this plan because they love people ... all people ... you ... very much!

Read more about it in **Isaiah 53**

ETERNAL LIFE

"I TELL YOU THE TRUTH, ANYONE WHO BELIEVES HAS ETERNAL LIFE."

JOHN 6:47

"Eternal" means forever – something that never ends. One of the promised blessings of accepting Jesus Christ as your Savior is the gift of eternal life. Now, you've probably noticed that in this life no one lives forever – everyone dies. So, what does eternal life mean?

Several Bible verses speak of what happens after a person's earthly life ends. In one verse Jesus said that He is preparing a place for His followers and it is a place where they can spend eternity. It is also mentioned that anyone who rejects Jesus as Savior will not be able to enter heaven and will spend forever with Satan in another place which we call hell.

Another thought on the topic of eternal life comes from John 6:47 which says that at the moment you believe you have eternal life. That means that the rest of your life on earth is fuller and richer with more meaning just because Jesus is a part of it.

Eternal life is living with Jesus in your life forever. While you're on this earth, He is with you and giving your life deeper meaning. When you die, you will join Him in heaven forever.

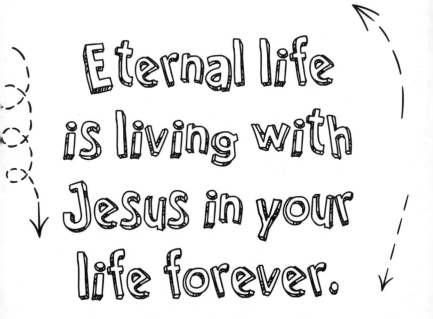

Eternal life is living with Jesus in your life forever.

What does the Bible say?

John 11:25

Jesus told her, "I am the resurrection and the life. Anyone who believes in Me will live, even after dying."

John 3:36

Anyone who believes in God's Son has eternal life. Anyone who doesn't obey the Son will never experience eternal life but remains under God's angry judgment.

John 5:24

"I tell you the truth, those who listen to My message and believe in God who sent Me have eternal life. They will never be condemned for their sins, but they have already passed from death into life."

1 John 5:11-12

And this is what God has testified: He has given us eternal life, and this life is in His Son. Whoever has the Son has life; whoever does not have God's Son does not have life.

Story About
Eternal Life

There are many questions about what heaven and hell will be like. Let's concentrate on heaven; the place Jesus has been getting ready for His followers.

Jesus' follower John tells us more than any other Bible writer about heaven. He describes a beautiful, holy city. He explains that it is a square 1,400 miles tall and wide. The walls around it are 216 feet thick and are made of a precious stone called jasper. The city itself is made of gold. The gates in the wall are made of huge pearls – each gate is just one complete pearl. The main street is made of pure gold that is as clear as glass.

There is no sun or moon because God's glory fills the city. There is no day or night. There is no evil and no sadness in this beautiful place because God is there and Jesus is there.

Only those who have accepted Jesus as Savior will be in this heaven.

> Read more about it in **Revelation 21**

GROWING IN FAITH

FAITH SHOWS THE REALITY OF WHAT WE HOPE FOR; IT IS THE EVIDENCE OF THINGS WE CANNOT SEE.

HEBREWS 11:1

Faith is basic to the Christian life. If you do not have faith you do not have a true relationship with God. But, what is faith? The Bible describes it in Hebrews 11:1 as the truth of all that you hope for but cannot currently see. Faith is proof that you trust in God.

Where do you get faith? It's not something you can create yourself. Faith is a gift from God. Your responsibility is to stay close to Him, read His Word and pray.

God sees what's in your heart. He knows if you really want to obey Him and please Him or if you're just sort of pretending for a while and will soon stop caring about Him. Truly wanting to please Him means you have faith; which means you trust Him completely and want to know Him better and better. It means you trust Him to care for you no matter what is happening in your life – even when difficult, painful things happen.

The Bible says that it is not possible to please God without having faith. It says that difficult times in your life teach you to trust God and that makes your faith stronger.

What does the Bible say?

Hebrews 11:6

It is impossible to please God without faith. Anyone who wants to come to Him must believe that God exists and that He rewards those who sincerely seek Him.

Ephesians 2:8-9

God saved you by His grace when you believed. And you can't take credit for this; it is a gift from God. Salvation is not a reward for the good things we have done, so none of us can boast about it.

1 Peter 1:8-9

You love Him even though you have never seen Him. Though you do not see Him now, you trust Him; and you rejoice with a glorious, inexpressible joy. The reward for trusting Him will be the salvation of your souls.

2 Corinthians 4:13-14

We continue to preach because we have the same kind of faith the psalmist had when he said, "I believed in God, so I spoke." We know that God, who raised the Lord Jesus, will also raise us with Jesus and present us to Himself together with you.

Faith Like No Other

One time an officer from the Roman army came to see Jesus. He was worried about his servant who was very sick. The young man was in a lot of pain and couldn't move. The officer wanted Jesus to heal the servant.

"I will come to your house and heal him," Jesus said.

But the Roman officer said, "Oh no. I'm not worthy of having You come to my house. I know that if You just say the words my servant will be healed. I know this because I am in charge of many soldiers. When I say, 'Do this or do that,' they do what I say."

Jesus was amazed at what this man said. He turned to the crowd of people following Him and said, "I have not seen faith as great as this in all of Israel and that's the truth!"

Then Jesus said to the officer, "Go on home. Your servant is healed." When the officer got home he found out that the servant was healed at the very time Jesus said those words!

Read more about it in Matthew 8:5-13

AMAZING grace

GOD SAVED YOU BY HIS GRACE WHEN YOU BELIEVED. AND YOU CAN'T TAKE CREDIT FOR THIS; IT IS A GIFT FROM GOD.

EPHESIANS 2:8

Grace is a major theme of the Christian life. What does the word "grace" mean? Grace means favor or blessing. When the Bible talks about God's grace to people it is recognizing that all people are sinners – everyone does things that are disobedient to God's laws and no one is completely pure as God is pure. But, instead of turning away from you, God chooses to save you and bless you and keep right on loving you. No one deserves His blessing and that's what makes it grace. The major theme of grace comes when you think of God saving you through salvation. He doesn't have to. You don't deserve His favor. He willingly gives it because He loves you so much.

Even after you are saved, God's grace is given to you day after day, in fact, many times throughout the day. Just think about how often you have a thought that is selfish or mean or judgmental toward another person. Each of those thoughts is sin and each time God extends grace to you by not turning away, and instead continuing to forgive and love. What an amazing gift is God's grace!

Amazing Grace!
How sweet the sound
that saved a wretch like me!
I once was lost,
but now I'm found;
was blind, but now I see.
JOHN NEWTON

What does the Bible say?

2 Corinthians 12:9

"My grace is all you need. My power works best in weakness."

Hebrews 4:16

So let us come boldly to the throne of our gracious God. There we will receive His mercy, and we will find grace to help us when we need it most.

Romans 3:24

God, in His grace, freely makes us right in His sight. He did this through Christ Jesus when He freed us from the penalty for our sins.

Romans 11:5-6

A few of the people of Israel have remained faithful because of God's grace – His undeserved kindness in choosing them. And since it is through God's kindness, then it is not by their good works. For in that case, God's grace would not be what it really is – free and undeserved.

The Fiery Furnace

King Nebuchadnezzar had a giant golden statue of himself set up. The people were to bow down and worship it each time they heard music. Many people did what the king ordered. But Shadrach, Meshach and Abednego refused to worship the king's statue. They would worship only the true God.

Shadrach, Meshach and Abednego were arrested and brought to the king. He gave them one more chance to obey his command. They refused and said, "Our God will rescue us from your punishment. But, even if He doesn't, we will never worship your statue."

The punishment for disobeying the king's order was to be thrown into a hot furnace. King Nebuchadnezzar angrily ordered, "Make the fire in the furnace seven times hotter! Then tie up these men and throw them into the fire."

Soldiers obeyed the king's orders and he sat down to watch the men die. But ... they didn't die. The king saw FOUR men walking around in the fire!

He had the three men taken out of the furnace. They were fine! They didn't even smell like smoke! The fourth man the king had seen was God's angel, sent to protect them. God, by His grace, saved Shadrach, Meshach and Abednego!

Read more about it in **Daniel 3**

REPENTANCE

NOW REPENT OF YOUR SINS AND TURN TO GOD, SO THAT YOUR SINS MAY BE WIPED AWAY.

ACTS 3:19

The word "repent" actually means to turn away from sin. When you repent it means you choose not to sin anymore, as much as is in your control. Of course, it is not possible to be completely sin free, but repenting of sins means you understand what God asks of you and you choose to believe that Jesus Christ is God and that He is your Savior. You are turning away from any disbelief in who He is and what He requires of you. When you believe that

Jesus is the Son of God and your Savior you become aware of your sinfulness and how much you need to turn away from your sin.

Repentance is an important part of salvation because it shows in the way you live. Your words and actions show that you understand that Jesus is God's Son and He died for your sins so you want to live your life in a way that pleases Him. You also spend time reading God's Word so you are learning how to obey Him and please Him.

Repentance makes a difference in your life because you have turned away from thinking your way is always best and only thinking of yourself. You want to live for God and obey Him.

Turn From   Turn To

Sin
Satan
Death

REPENTANCE

Salvation
God
Life

What does the Bible say?

Luke 3:8

Prove by the way you live that you have repented of your sins and turned to God.

Acts 2:38

Peter replied, "Each of you must repent of your sins and turn to God, and be baptized in the name of Jesus Christ for the forgiveness of your sins. Then you will receive the gift of the Holy Spirit.

Acts 3:19

Repent of your sins and turn to God, so that your sins may be wiped away.

Romans 2:4

Don't you see how wonderfully kind, tolerant, and patient God is with you? Does this mean nothing to you? Can't you see that His kindness is intended to turn you from your sin?

Saul Repents

Saul wanted all Christians – people who believed Jesus was the Son of God – put into prison. He dedicated his life to rounding up the Christians and putting them in jail.

Saul was on his way to the town of Damascus to attack the Christians there. He was traveling with some other people. Suddenly a bright light shined down on Saul and a voice asked, "Why are you persecuting Me?"

Saul fell to the ground and asked, "Who are You?"

The voice answered, "I am Jesus. The One you are persecuting. Get up and go into the city and wait for Me to tell you what to do."

When Saul got up, he couldn't see so his friends had to lead him into the city.

Read more about it in Acts 9

That experience changed Saul's heart. After Jesus spoke to him Saul repented and turned his life's work to traveling and sharing the message of God's love and Jesus' sacrifice.

CONFESSING YOUR SIN

IF WE CONFESS OUR SINS TO HIM, HE IS FAITHFUL AND JUST TO FORGIVE US OUR SINS AND TO CLEANSE US FROM ALL WICKEDNESS.

1 JOHN 1:9

Confessing your sin means admitting your sin to God and to yourself. Confessing is saying, "I did this. I'm guilty. I'm sorry for it."

When you accept Jesus as your Savior, your sins are forgiven. So, why do you need to do any more confessing after that point? The most important reason for confessing is that God tells you to. The verse above promises that confession brings God's forgiveness.

When you confess your sins it shows that you understand you have disobeyed God. It makes you own your sin. You speak it to God and to yourself so there is no denying it or blaming it on anyone else. So, confessing is sort of like a daily clean-up of your heart. It keeps you in good standing with God.

It's not possible to have a good relationship with God if you have unconfessed sin in your heart. Set aside a time each day, maybe each night, to confess your sins, ask forgiveness and then start the next day fresh with God.

What does the Bible say?

Psalm 103:12

He has removed our sins as far from us as the east is from the west.

Romans 14:11

"'As surely as I live,' says the LORD, 'every knee will bend to Me, and every tongue will declare allegiance to God.'"

Luke 12:8

"I tell you the truth, everyone who acknowledges Me publicly here on earth, the Son of Man will also acknowledge in the presence of God's angels."

1 John 1:9

If we confess our sins to God, He can always be trusted to forgive us and take our sins away.

A Biblical Example of Confession

God said that David was a "man after God's own heart." God even chose David to lead His people. David tried to obey God and live for Him. He really wanted to and God knew that because He looked at David's heart and saw David's desire to please Him. However, sometimes David made bad choices and did things that didn't please God.

When David disobeyed God, he confessed his sin and asked God's forgiveness. He didn't try to blame his sin on anyone else. David accepted the responsibility for his choices. He confessed his sin and asked God's forgiveness.

Read about David's confession in **Psalm 32**

THE LORD'S SUPPER

EVERY TIME YOU EAT THIS BREAD AND DRINK THIS CUP, YOU ARE ANNOUNCING THE LORD'S DEATH UNTIL HE COMES AGAIN.

I CORINTHIANS 11:26

The Lord's Supper is also called Communion or Eucharist. It is a sacrament of the Christian faith that Jesus established near the end of His life on earth.

Jesus gathered His disciples in an upper room to celebrate the Passover Feast shortly before He was arrested and crucified. This last meal with His friends has come to be known as the Last Supper. Jesus broke a loaf of bread into pieces and shared it with His friends. Then He shared wine with them. As He gave them these things He said, "This bread is My body, broken for you. This wine is My blood, spilled for you. Whenever you eat this bread or drink this cup, remember Me." He was telling them that He would die soon and that His death was a gift to them, which would make a close relationship with God possible.

Communion or The Lord's Supper is observed now by Christians eating a small piece of bread and drinking a little wine or juice as they remember Jesus' sacrifice. It's meant to be a time of reflection and confession – a time of renewal.

What does the Bible say?

Psalm 19:14

May the words of my mouth and the meditation of my heart be pleasing to You, O LORD, my rock and my redeemer.

James 4:8

Come close to God, and God will come close to you. Wash your hands, you sinners; purify your hearts, for your loyalty is divided between God and the world.

Titus 3:5

He saved us, not because of the righteous things we had done, but because of His mercy. He washed away our sins, giving us a new birth and new life through the Holy Spirit.

Philippians 2:7-8

He gave up His divine privileges; He took the humble position of a slave and was born as a human being. When He appeared in human form, He humbled Himself in obedience to God and died a criminal's death on a cross.

The First Last Supper

Jesus' ministry on earth was only for 3 ½ years. He knew that His earthly life was about to come to a close and, of course, He made good use of His time with His followers. The Passover Feast was an important observation for the Hebrew people of God's protection of His people when He led them out of slavery in Egypt. As time for the celebration approached, Jesus sent two disciples into Jerusalem to prepare the dinner.

When everything was ready, Jesus and His twelve disciples sat down to share the Passover meal together. As they ate, Jesus took a loaf of bread and broke it into pieces. He said, "This bread is My body which will be broken for you," as He passed the bread out to each of them. Then He poured wine for them and said, "This is My blood which is shed for you. Every time you have this meal, think about Me and My sacrifice for you."

Read more about the Last Supper in Matthew 26:17-30

WHAT IS BAPTISM?

"GO AND MAKE DISCIPLES OF ALL THE NATIONS, BAPTIZING THEM IN THE NAME OF THE FATHER AND THE SON AND THE HOLY SPIRIT."

MATTHEW 28:19

Baptism is an ordinance, or decree that Jesus set for the church. It is one way a Christian publicly shows his decision to follow Jesus. While baptism is not required for salvation, it is an act of obedience since Jesus instructed the church to baptize believers.

Baptism is an illustration of Jesus' death, burial and resurrection as a person is lowered under the water and then lifted from it. Baptism publicly signifies a person's commitment of death to sin and the rising to new life in Christ.

The experience of baptism shows obedience to Christ once a person has accepted salvation through Christ's death and resurrection. It also shows unity with Christian believers who have also followed Christ in baptism.

What does the Bible say?

Mark 1:9-11

One day Jesus came from Nazareth in Galilee, and John baptized Him in the Jordan River. As Jesus came up out of the water, He saw the heavens splitting apart and the Holy Spirit descending on Him like a dove. And a voice from heaven said, "You are My dearly loved Son, and You bring Me great joy."

Mark 16:16

"Anyone who believes and is baptized will be saved."

Acts 2:38

Peter replied, "Each of you must repent of your sins and turn to God, and be baptized in the name of Jesus Christ for the forgiveness of your sins. Then you will receive the gift of the Holy Spirit."

1 Corinthians 12:13

Some of us are Jews, some are Gentiles, some are slaves, and some are free. But we have all been baptized into one body by one Spirit, and we all share the same Spirit.

The Baptism
of Jesus

Many people came to John the Baptist to be baptized in the Jordan River. He told them that while he baptized them with water someone would come later who would baptize them with the Holy Spirit. He was talking about Jesus. To John's surprise, one day Jesus, Himself, came to John to be baptized. John said, "I'm not worthy to baptize You! You should baptize me."

But Jesus knew what Scripture said and He knew that He needed to be baptized by John to fulfill what had been predicted. So, John lowered Jesus into the water then lifted Him up. As Jesus came up out of the water, the Spirit of God came from heaven looking like a dove and landed on Him. A voice from heaven said, "This is My dear Son whom I love. I am very pleased with Him."

Read the whole story in Matthew 3:13-17

WHAT IS HEAVEN?

"HEAVEN IS MY THRONE, AND THE EARTH IS MY FOOTSTOOL. COULD YOU BUILD ME A TEMPLE AS GOOD AS THAT?" ASKS THE LORD.

ACTS 7:49

Heaven is where God's throne is. The Bible tells us that after Jesus was resurrected from the dead, He was taken up to heaven and sat at God's right hand, the place of honor.

Heaven is the place where God's children will spend eternity with Him. Jesus promised that when He left earth He would go to heaven to prepare a place for

His friends to be with Him forever. He will come back to earth one day and take His followers to heaven with Him. It is a real place, though it may exist in a different form from life on this earth.

The apostle John was blessed to see heaven and be able to write about it in the Bible. Not much other concrete information about heaven is given in the Bible, except that it is promised to be a wonderful place filled with reward and blessing for those who have served and obeyed God. Best of all … believers will be with Him for eternity!

What does the Bible say?

John 14:2-3

"There is more than enough room in My Father's home. If this were not so, would I have told you that I am going to prepare a place for you? When everything is ready, I will come and get you, so that you will always be with Me where I am."

Revelation 21:1-2

Then I saw a new heaven and a new earth, for the old heaven and the old earth had disappeared. And the sea was also gone. And I saw the holy city, the new Jerusalem, coming down from God out of heaven like a bride beautifully dressed for her husband.

Philippians 3:20-21

We are citizens of heaven, where the Lord Jesus Christ lives. And we are eagerly waiting for Him to return as our Savior. He will take our weak mortal bodies and change them into glorious bodies like His own, using the same power with which He will bring everything under His control.

What Is Heaven Like?

John was banned to the island of Patmos but while he was there God allowed him to have a vision of heaven. He wrote that God was there in all His glory. He said that there is no night in heaven because God is light and His light fills heaven so the sun and moon are no longer needed. The city is filled with wonderful gemstones that shimmer and glow. It is more beautiful than anything you can imagine.

There are no tears or sorrow in heaven. There is no loneliness because there is no death and God's presence is always there. In heaven believers will know true love because they will be with Jesus who loved them enough to die for them and who has been in heaven since His resurrection, making place for believers to be with Him forever.

Read more about it in Revelation 21

WHO IS SATAN?

SATAN, WHO IS THE GOD OF THIS WORLD, HAS BLINDED THE MINDS OF THOSE WHO DON'T BELIEVE. THEY ARE UNABLE TO SEE THE GLORIOUS LIGHT OF THE GOOD NEWS. THEY DON'T UNDERSTAND THIS MESSAGE ABOUT THE GLORY OF CHRIST, WHO IS THE EXACT LIKENESS OF GOD.

2 CORINTHIANS 4:4

The Bible tells us that Satan was a holy angel created by God. His original name may have been Lucifer. He was a very beautiful angel and one of the highest created beings in the angel world. But Satan became filled with pride because of his own beauty and importance and thought he was more important than God so he wanted to rule instead of obey.

The first time Satan is seen in the Bible is in the Garden of Eden when, disguised as a serpent, he gets Eve and Adam to disobey God and taste the fruit they had been told not to eat.

God removed Satan from his important position and they became enemies. He's now the ruler of this earthly world and the prince of the power of the air. He makes every effort to pull people away from God. He accuses God of bad things. He places doubts in the minds of people. He tricks and lies to people. He does whatever he can to get people to worship him instead of God. He can try all he wants, but on Judgment Day, God will do away with Satan forever and cast him in the lake of fire forever.

What does the Bible say?

Isaiah 14:12

How you are fallen from heaven, O shining star, son of the morning! You have been thrown down to the earth, you who destroyed the nations of the world.

Ephesians 2:1-2

Once you were dead because of your disobedience and your many sins. You used to live in sin, just like the rest of the world, obeying the devil. He is the spirit at work in the hearts of those who refuse to obey God.

John 12:31

"The time for judging this world has come, when Satan, the ruler of this world, will be cast out."

Ephesians 6:11

Put on all of God's armor so that you will be able to stand firm against all strategies of the devil.

1 Peter 5:8

Stay alert! Watch out for your great enemy, the devil. He prowls around like a roaring lion, looking for someone to devour.

The End of Satan

This is what John wrote about God's victory over Satan:

Then I saw an angel coming down from heaven with the key to the bottomless pit and a heavy chain in his hand. He seized the dragon – that old serpent, who is the devil, Satan – and bound him in chains for a thousand years. The angel threw him into the bottomless pit, which he then shut and locked so Satan could not deceive the nations anymore until the thousand years were finished. Afterward he must be released for a little while.

When the thousand years come to an end, Satan will be let out of his prison. He will go out to deceive the nations – called Gog and Magog – in every corner of the earth. He will gather them together for battle – a mighty army, as numberless as sand along the seashore. And I saw them as they went up on the broad plain of the earth and surrounded God's people and the beloved city. But fire from heaven came down on the attacking armies and consumed them. Then the devil, who had deceived them, was thrown into the fiery lake of burning sulfur, joining the beast and the false prophet. There they will be tormented day and night forever and ever.

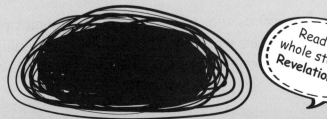

Read the whole story in **Revelation 20**

IS HELL A REAL PLACE?

... WHEN THE LORD JESUS APPEARS FROM HEAVEN. HE WILL COME WITH HIS MIGHTY ANGELS, IN FLAMING FIRE, BRINGING JUDGMENT ON THOSE WHO DON'T KNOW GOD AND ON THOSE WHO REFUSE TO OBEY THE GOOD NEWS OF OUR LORD JESUS. THEY WILL BE PUNISHED WITH ETERNAL DESTRUCTION, FOREVER SEPARATED FROM THE LORD AND FROM HIS GLORIOUS POWER.

2 THESSALONIANS 1:7-9

Yes, hell is just as real as heaven is. Many times as He taught, Jesus warned people about the reality and danger of rejecting God and being condemned to hell.

God gives each person who lives on earth the opportunity to choose to follow Him or not. Those who do will be welcomed into His heaven to be with Him for all of eternity. Those who do not will be condemned to hell, a place of torment and horror.

The Bible does not give us a lot of details as to what hell is like except that it means complete separation from God forever. Since God is light and love and good it is fair to think that hell will be just the opposite of those things without His presence there. Hell will be a place that is like Satan, evil, dark, unhappy and tormented.

What does the Bible say?

Psalm 9:17

The wicked will go down to the grave. This is the fate of all the nations who ignore God.

Mark 9:43

"If your hand causes you to sin, cut it off. It's better to enter eternal life with only one hand than to go into the unquenchable fires of hell with two hands."

Matthew 25:41

"The King will turn to those on the left and say, 'Away with you, you cursed ones, into the eternal fire prepared for the devil and his demons.'"

2 Peter 2:4

God did not spare even the angels who sinned. He threw them into hell, in gloomy pits of darkness, where they are being held until the day of judgment.

The Reality
of Hell

Jesus told the story of a rich man who had everything he needed – plenty of food, a nice home and beautiful clothes. A poor man named Lazarus lay on the ground outside the home of the rich man. His body was covered with sores. He was hungry and longed for scraps of food from the rich man's table.

Finally the poor man died and angels came and carried him away to heaven where he sat beside the great Father Abraham. Not long after that the rich man died, too. But he was carried away to hell where he was in torment day and night. Off in the distance the rich man could see Abraham and Lazarus. He cried out to them, asking that Abraham let Lazarus go back to earth to warn the rich man's family about the pain of hell.

Abraham said, "Moses and the prophets have already warned them."

The rich man said, "They might listen to one who is warning them from this place himself."

But Abraham said, "If they wouldn't listen to Moses, they will not listen to anyone."

Read more about this story in **Luke 16:19-31**

GOD'S ANGELS

HE WILL ORDER HIS ANGELS TO PROTECT YOU WHEREVER YOU GO.

PSALM 91:11

The Bible speaks of angels as real, created beings who serve God. Different angels have different responsibilities. It seems most likely that angels are not sweet creatures with halos and wings as we often picture them, but are strong and powerful as they do God's work.

Most of the time when we read of angels appearing in the Bible, people react with fear and trembling.

This could be because it was not common to see an angel or because their appearance commanded great respect.

The word "angel" comes from a Greek word that means "messenger" so we know that angels deliver God's messages to people.

Two angels are named in Scripture. Michael is the archangel, which may mean that he is over all the other angels. Gabriel is an angel who brought messages to people in Scripture. Other angels are called cherubim and seraphim who seem to have the purpose of praising and glorifying God.

What does the Bible say?

Deuteronomy 32:43

Rejoice with Him, you heavens, and let all of God's angels worship Him. Rejoice with His people, you Gentiles, and let all the angels be strengthened in Him.

Nehemiah 9:6

"You alone are the LORD. You made the skies and the heavens and all the stars. You made the earth and the seas and everything in them. You preserve them all, and the angels of heaven worship you.

Matthew 24:31

"He will send out His angels with the mighty blast of a trumpet, and they will gather His chosen ones from all over the world – from the farthest ends of the earth and heaven."

Luke 2:13-14

Suddenly, the angel was joined by a vast host of others – the armies of heaven – praising God and saying, "Glory to God in highest heaven and peace on earth to those with whom God is pleased."

A Special
Angel Message

Mary was a young Hebrew woman who tried to obey and honor God in all she said and did. God noticed that and He was pleased with her. So one day He sent His special messenger angel, Gabriel, to give Mary some important news.

"Mary, God is very pleased with you. He wants you to know that you are going to have a baby – a Son. You will name Him Jesus. He will be very great and will be called the Son of the Most High God. He will reign over Israel forever. His kingdom will never come to an end."

Mary was confused because she wasn't even married. How could she have a baby?

Gabriel said, "The power of the Holy Spirit will come on you. The baby you will have will be holy and will be called God's own Son."

Mary said, "I want to serve God. May everything you have told me come to be." Then Gabriel left her.

Read more about it in Luke 1:26-38

PRAYER

DON'T WORRY ABOUT ANYTHING; INSTEAD, PRAY ABOUT EVERY-THING. TELL GOD WHAT YOU NEED, AND THANK HIM FOR ALL HE HAS DONE. THEN YOU WILL EXPERIENCE GOD'S PEACE, WHICH EXCEEDS ANYTHING WE CAN UNDERSTAND. HIS PEACE WILL GUARD YOUR HEARTS AND MINDS AS YOU LIVE IN CHRIST JESUS.

PHILIPPIANS 4:6-7

Prayer is an amazing privilege we are invited to share in. God Himself asks us to pray to Him. What is prayer? Prayer is simply the experience of talking with God. He invites us to tell Him anything that is on our minds, anything we are worried about; anything we need His help with; anything we want to ask Him to do. Prayer is talking with Him and trusting Him to listen. He promised that He would. Since prayer is a conversation, there is not a right or wrong way to pray though we are instructed to pray "in Jesus' name" and it's always a good idea to confess sins so that we pray with a clean heart.

Different kinds of prayers are intercessory – prayer for someone else, supplication, requests, prayers of thanksgiving and prayers of worship. When we pray we confess to God that we know He is greater than we are. We acknowledge His power and His love by making our requests known to Him.

WHEN YOU PRAY, THINK OF:

J ESUS (THANK HIM + WORSHIP HIM)

O THERS (PRAY FOR FAMILY, FRIENDS)

Y OU (THEN LASTLY FOR YOURSELF)

What does the Bible Say?

1 Thessalonians 5:17

Never stop praying.

Matthew 7:7

"Keep on asking, and you will receive what you ask for. Keep on seeking, and you will find. Keep on knocking, and the door will be opened to you."

Ephesians 6:18

Pray in the Spirit at all times and on every occasion. Stay alert and be persistent in your prayers for all believers everywhere.

Matthew 6:6

"When you pray, go away by yourself, shut the door behind you, and pray to your Father in private. Then your Father, who sees everything, will reward you."

James 5:16

The earnest prayer of a righteous person has great power.

A Prayer Example

A big part of Jesus' ministry on earth was spent teaching His followers how to live for God and how to grow their faith. His example of knowing God included many times when He went off by Himself to pray.

One time a follower asked Jesus to teach them how to pray. This is what Jesus taught them:

Our Father in heaven,
hallowed be Your name.
Your kingdom come.
Your will be done on earth
as it is in heaven.
Give us this day our daily bread.
And forgive us our debts,
as we forgive our debtors.
And do not lead us into temptation,
but deliver us from the evil one.
For Yours is the kingdom
and the power
and the glory forever.
Amen.

Read more about this in Matthew 6:9-13 or Luke 11:2-4

MY FAVORITE BIBLE VERSES